The Mighty Mississippi

Contents

Rigby®

A Harcourt Achieve Imprint

www.Rigby.com
1-800-531-5015

Where Does the River Begin?

The Mississippi River begins at Lake Itasca where it is only a small stream. It is about 12 feet wide and less than 2 feet deep.

HERE 1475 FT
ABOVE
THE OCEAN
THE MIGHTY
MISSISSIPPI
BEGINS
TO FLOW
ON ITS
WINDING WAY
2552 MILES
TO THE
GULF OF
MEXICO

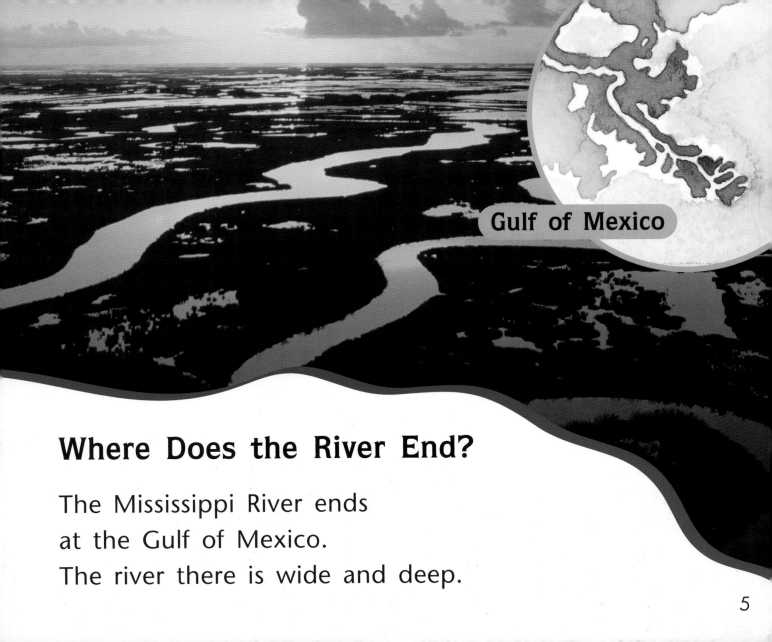

Gulf of Mexico

Where Does the River End?

The Mississippi River ends
at the Gulf of Mexico.
The river there is wide and deep.

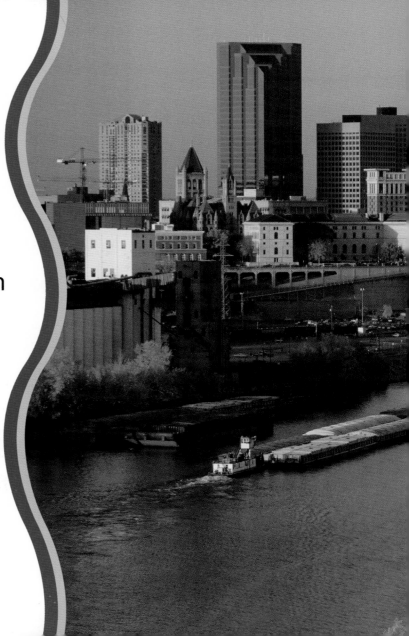

Who Lives near the Mississippi River?

Some people live and work in big cities along the Mississippi River.

Sometimes they have fun near the river.

Many farmers live near
the Mississippi River, too.
Some of them grow food
for people in the cities.

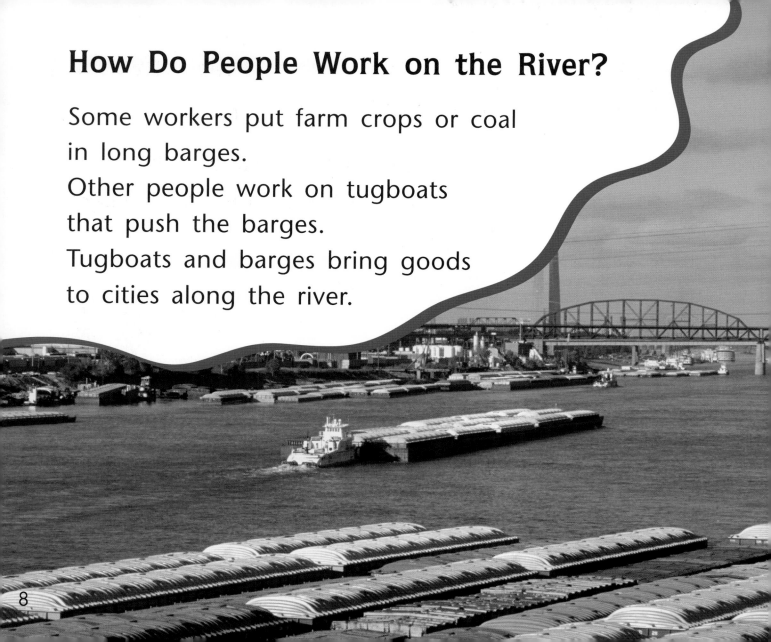

How Do People Work on the River?

Some workers put farm crops or coal
in long barges.
Other people work on tugboats
that push the barges.
Tugboats and barges bring goods
to cities along the river.

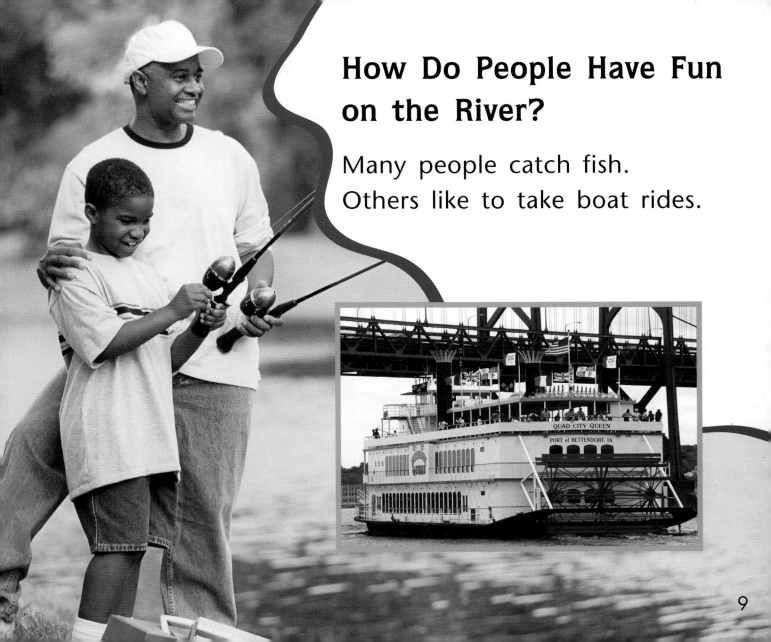

How Do People Have Fun on the River?

Many people catch fish.
Others like to take boat rides.

What Animals Live near the Mississippi River?

Ducks and geese build nests near the Mississippi River. Pelicans with big bills and herons with long legs live there, too.

Four-legged animals also have homes near the river. Some of them are opossums and muskrats.

When Does the Mississippi River Flood?

Water from melted snow
or heavy rain runs
into the river.
A river floods
when all of this water
spills out over the land.

People try to stop floods on the Mississippi River. They fill bags with sand and place the sandbags along the flooding river.

What Happens When the River Floods?

In towns and cities, flood water and mud cover the streets. Of course, then people must clean their houses and stores.

A flood can also kill a farmer's crops. But when the flood is over, the land can grow more crops.

The river can hurt and help us.
That's why people say it's the Mighty Mississippi.

Index